Written for children just like
William George Gajendran.
'... Jesus said,
"Let the little children come to me
and do not hinder them,
for to such belongs the kingdom of heaven."'
(Matthew 19:14)
I0816261

10 9 8 7 6 5 4 3 2 1

ISBN: 978-1-5271-1221-6

Published by Christian Focus Publications,
Geanies House, Fearn, Tain, Ross-shire, IV20 1TW, U.K.

Illustrations by Daniele Fabbri.
Printed and bound by Akcent Media, the Czech Republic

Scripture quotations are author's own paraphrases, unless otherwise stated.

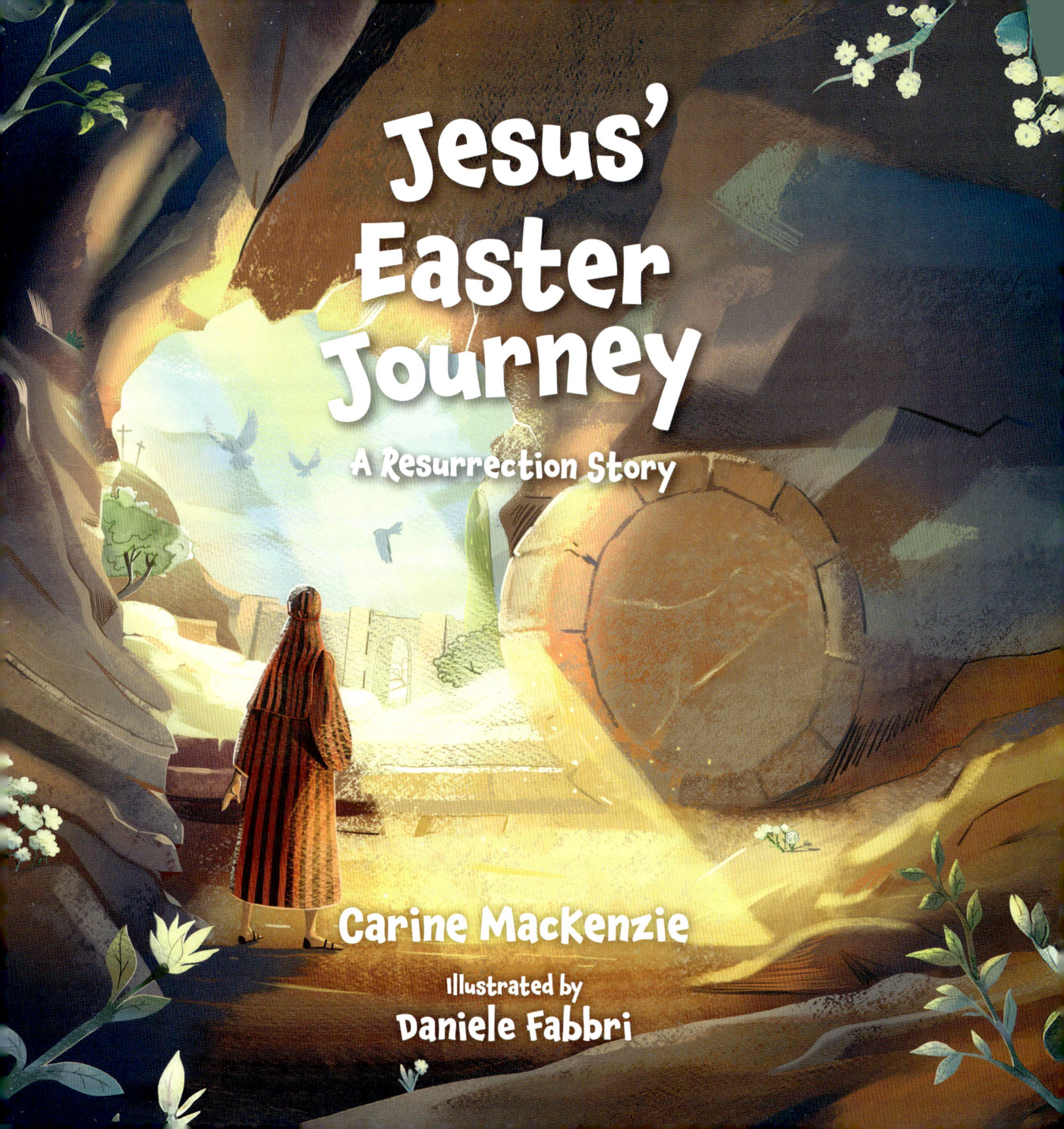
Jesus' Easter Journey
A Resurrection Story
Carine MacKenzie
Illustrated by
Daniele Fabbri

On the road to Jerusalem, Jesus stopped at the Mount of Olives overlooking the city.
'Go to that village over there,' he told two of his disciples.
'You will find a young donkey. Bring it to me.'
The disciples brought the young donkey and put some of their clothes on its back.

Jesus rode into Jerusalem, and crowds of people joined the procession. Some cut down branches from palm trees and placed them on the ground in front of Jesus. Others laid down their cloaks. The crowd shouted out joyfully, 'Hosanna to the Son of David. Blessed is he that comes in the name of the Lord.' Jesus rode right into the town.

The next day, Jesus' journey took him to the temple. There he chased away the greedy men who were using the temple as a trading place. The little children sang, praised, and cheered Jesus. He made blind people see and lame people walk. The chief priests and teachers of the law were not pleased to hear the children singing and cheering. But Jesus was pleased to hear them praising him.

It was time for the Passover feast. Jesus sent two of his disciples ahead to get ready for it. 'Follow the man you will meet, who will be carrying a jar of water,' said Jesus. 'He will lead you to a house. Explain to the owner that we need a room in which to eat the Passover feast. He will show you to a large upstairs room. Get everything ready there.' They followed his instructions, and in the evening, Jesus arrived with the rest of the disciples.

The Passover feast took on a new meaning that night. Jesus was preparing himself and his followers for his death. He broke the bread and handed it around. 'This is my body,' he said. Then he passed around a cup of wine and said, 'This is my blood. When you eat the bread and drink the wine, remember me.'

We call this the Lord's Supper.
Followers of Jesus all over the world, remember him in this way still.

Jesus went to pray in a garden called Gethsemane.
He took Peter, James and John with him.
'I am troubled,' he said. 'Stay here and keep me company.'
He went a little further on and prayed to God his Father. When he came back the disciples were sleeping. All the worry had exhausted them.
'Why are you sleeping?' Jesus asked. 'Get up and pray.'

While he was still speaking, Judas Iscariot and a crowd of men approached them. Judas had made an agreement with Jesus' enemies. They had given him money to hand Jesus over to them. When the disciples saw what was happening, they wanted to fight. One of them lashed out with a sword and cut off the ear of the high priest's servant. But Jesus touched the man's ear and it was immediately healed. Jesus was then led away to the high priest's house.

Peter followed the crowd at a distance.
While Jesus was being questioned and bullied in the high priest's house, Peter stayed in the courtyard. He warmed himself by the fire. A servant girl peered at him.
'This man was with Jesus,' she said.
'I don't know him,' Peter exclaimed.
Later, someone else said, 'You are one of them.'
'I am not,' said Peter hotly.
Then someone said, 'This man was with Jesus – he is a Galilean.'
'I don't know what you are talking about,' declared Peter.

Just then a cockerel crowed at daybreak. Jesus looked over to Peter and caught his eye. How ashamed Peter felt. He went out and wept bitterly. He had let Jesus down. He had denied him.

Jesus' journey was not over. He was sent to Pilate, the Roman Governor.
'Are you the King of the Jews?' Pilate asked.
'Yes, that is so,' replied Jesus.
'I do not find any fault with this man,' declared Pilate.
'But he is raising trouble in the whole country!' was the claim.
When Pilate heard that Jesus was from Galilee, he packed him off to Herod, the ruler. Herod was pleased to see Jesus at last and asked him many questions.
But Jesus was silent.

Herod and the soldiers cruelly mocked him. They dressed him up in a purple robe and then sent him back to Pilate. Pilate could still find no fault.

'I have the power to release one prisoner during the Passover week. I could release Jesus,' he suggested.

'No!' shouted the crowd. 'We do not want you to release Jesus. We want you to release Barabbas, the criminal.'

Jesus was led away to be crucified. This was a cruel death – being nailed to a wooden cross. He was not angry. He prayed to God saying, 'Father, forgive them, for they do not realise what they are doing.'

He asked his disciple, John, to look after Mary as if she were his own mother.

Two thieves were crucified along with Jesus. One of them knew he deserved his punishment and realised that Jesus was the Son of God. 'Remember me when you come to your kingdom,' he said. Jesus promised, 'Today you will be with me in paradise.' In the final moments of his life, this thief asked Jesus for mercy. Jesus showed him love by forgiving his sin.

From twelve noon until three o'clock in the afternoon,
there was darkness over at the whole land. How frightening!
Jesus was bearing the full punishment for all the sins of his people.
'Why have you left me alone?' he called out to God, his Father, in agony.
Just before he died, he shouted out with a loud voice,
'Father, into your hands I commit my spirit.'

The big, thick curtain in the temple was torn from the top to the bottom. The earth quaked and rocks were split open. These miraculous events amazed the soldiers and others standing by. 'This was certainly the son of God,' they declared.

That evening, a rich man called Joseph went boldly to Pilate and asked permission to bury Jesus' body. Joseph and his friend Nicodemus carefully took Jesus' body down from the cross and wrapped it in a linen cloth. They then placed his body in a tomb in a garden. This was a large cave cut out of the rock. A big stone was placed at the mouth of the cave like a door. The big stone was sealed, and guardsmen were told to keep watch.

How sad Jesus' friends must have felt that Sabbath day.
Jesus was dead. What would happen next?

Early in the morning of the first day of the week (we call it Sunday), some women came to the tomb. When they reached the tomb, what a surprise they got. The stone was rolled away, and an angel was sitting on it. Jesus' body was not in the tomb. One of the women ran to tell Peter and John what had happened. The others looked inside the tomb and found two angels.

'Do not be afraid,' one said. 'I know you are looking for Jesus. Do not look for him here. He is risen from the dead.'

The first person to see the risen Lord Jesus was Mary Magdalene. She was weeping in the garden and spoke to a man she thought was the gardener. The man spoke her name, 'Mary!' and she immediately realised that he was Jesus. Mary ran with the good news to the disciples. In the days that followed, Jesus appeared to all the disciples and many others too. When he came into the room where the disciples were hiding, they were terrified, but he said to them, 'Peace be with you.'

Cleopas and his friend were walking along the road to Emmaus, talking about all that had happened in Jerusalem during the past few days. They were upset at how events had turned out.

Jesus came alongside them and walked with him, but they did not recognise him. They thought he was a stranger. Jesus explained, from the Old Testament, all that had happened to himself.

When they reached Emmaus,
they persuaded Jesus to come into the house for some food, for it was late.

When they sat down for supper,
Jesus took the bread, blessed it and handed them a piece.
Just then they realised that he was the risen Lord Jesus.
He disappeared from their sight.
They then understood all that had been said on the road.
They rushed back to Jerusalem to tell the disciples.
'The Lord really has risen,' they said.

Sometime later, seven of the disciples went fishing on the Sea of Galilee. They fished all night but caught nothing. On their return, they noticed a man standing on the beach. This was in fact Jesus, but they did not know that.

'Have you anything to eat?' the man asked.

'No!' they replied.

'Put your net down again,' he said.

When they did that, they caught a huge number of fish.

John then recognised Jesus. 'It is the Lord,' he said to Peter. Peter jumped into the sea to rush ashore ahead of the boat.

On the shore, Jesus had a fire ready with some cooked fish and bread. They had a lovely breakfast together.

Jesus' journey on earth was nearly at an end. Jesus and his disciples left the city for the Mount of Olives. Jesus told his disciples that they would be his witnesses at home, and in many places, telling others the good news of the gospel. He blessed them and was lifted up into heaven, right through the clouds. The disciples stood gazing up into the sky where Jesus had gone.

Two men in white clothes stood beside them. 'Why are you standing there staring? Just as you have seen Jesus being taken up into heaven, he will return to earth one day.' This filled the disciples with joy. They went to work with new energy, praising God and preaching his word everywhere they went.

Followers of Jesus are still telling this wonderful story all over the world today. This is the most important event in history. We can have new life if we trust that what he has done for us on the cross has paid the price for our sins. This is the good news of the gospel. We must believe it and pass it on to others. Those who believe in Jesus know that his journey is not over yet. One day in the future he will return. He will come as a victorious king and judge. Every knee will bow and every one will confess that Jesus is Lord.

Christian Focus is for Kids

That means you and your friends can all find a book to help you from the CF4KIDS range – from the very littlest baby to kids that are almost too old to be called a kid anymore.

We publish books that introduce you to the real Jesus, the truth of God's Word, and what that means for boys and girls of all ages.

Reading books is a fun way to find out what it is like to be a follower of Jesus Christ.

True stories, adventures, activity books, and devotions – they are all here for you and your family.

Christian Focus is part of the family of God. We aim to glorify Jesus and help you trust and follow Him.

Christian Focus Publications Ltd,
Geanies House, Fearn, Ross-shire,
IV20 1TW, Scotland,
United Kingdom.
www.christianfocus.com